Yoga

For Your Sex Life

Monique Joiner Siedlak

OSHUN
PUBLICATIONS

Printed in the United States of America

Second Edition 2018

ISBN-13: 978-1-948834-62-9

Publisher
www.oshunpublications.com

Disclaimer
All the material contained in this book is provided for educational and informational purposes only. No responsibility can be taken for any results or outcomes resulting from the use of this material. While every attempt has been made to provide information that is both accurate and effective, the author does not assume any responsibility for the accuracy or use/misuse of this information.

Notice

This book is not intended as a substitute for the medical advice of physicians. The reader should regularly consult a physician or therapist in matters relating to his/her health and particularly with respect to any symptoms that may require diagnosis or medical attention.

Yoga Poses Photos

Pixabay.com

Freepik.com

Dreamstime.com

Cover Design by Monique Joiner Siedlak

Cover Image by Pixabay.com

Logo Design by Monique Joiner Siedlak

Logo Image by Pixabay.com

Sign up to email list: www.mojosiedlak.com

Other Books in the Series

Yoga for Beginners

Yoga for Stress

Yoga for Back Pain

Yoga for Weight Loss

Yoga for Flexibility

Yoga for Advanced Beginners

Yoga for Fitness

Yoga for Runners

Yoga for Energy

Yoga: To Beat Depression and Anxiety

Yoga for Menstruation

Table of Contents

Introduction

Yoga is wonderful. It encourages you to find harmony in your life. By showing us to take advantage of each point and experience life one breath at a time, yoga lets us better relate with ourselves and our partner.

Yoga tones up our bodies, reduce our stress levels, and develop our energy, but did you know yoga can likewise help fire up your sexuality and your sex life?

These poses are for the beginners and experienced. With a constant habit, they'll improve flexibility and heighten body awareness and self-confidence, all of which make you happier in your own skin, meaning you're more prone to get relaxed and confident in an intimate relationship.

A good sex life is not merely a great way to keep yourself sexually satisfied but is also great for your body shape and weight, for keeping your heart healthy, your blood pressure low and even for increasing your own libido. Sex is also excellent for boosting your immune system and protecting yourself against some of the most common ailments, such as flu.

Unfortunately, there is a significant number of problems that can arise in any of the two partners involved that causes sex to become less pleasurable or even less frequent. When these problems arise, the two partners can lose interest in each other, since sex is a particular activity that keeps an intimate bond between two partners strong. When sex is not as good as it used to be any longer, that intimate bond may slowly start to wither away. Yoga poses for healthy sex can help a couple to conquer the sexual issues between the couple.

Cat Pose (Marjariasana)

The Cat Pose consists of relaxation of your back by taking on a posture of a cat. It is generally used to begin a yoga exercise, following the initial establishment of breath, by going through cat and cow pose. Amidst a nice steady foundation in tabletop, this movement allows us grounding as we begin to gently open up the back body and stimulate the core. It's most indispensable goal, though, is the opportunity it enables to combine the breath with activity.

How to Do

Start off by placing yourself in a tabletop position, using your hands and knees as the four legs of a table. Your knees would be positioned up and down below your hips. Your shoulders, wrists, and elbows should be parallel and perpendicular to the ground. You will then focus your eyes on the floor, with your head in a middle position.

Let your breath out and allow your spine to curve by directing it upward to the ceiling. Your shoulders and knees should be in the recommended four-legged position. At this moment, let your head somewhat fall towards the floor. Do not fall so far that your chin is pressed into the sternal hollow of your chest.

While inhaling, once again come back to the typical tabletop position. Maintain breathing in and breathing out deeply while transferring your position from relaxed to alert. Maintain until you feel the relaxation in your spine.

Benefits

The Cat Pose gradually works your spine as well as its muscles. It stretches your neck, back, and torso. In addition to improving the functions of your belly organs, it calms your mind by alleviating it from tension and stress.

Tips

The Cat Pose is an easy and simple yoga pose to relax your fatigued body. Ask your partner or friend to lay a hand in the middle of your shoulder blades if you are finding it challenging to bring a curve in the upper section of your back which will then result in a prompt triggering of that area.

Cow Pose (Bitilasana)

The Cow Pose is regularly instructed in sequence with the Cat Pose to do a mild warm-up sequence. When practiced together, the poses help to stretch the body and prepare it for other activity.

You will inhale through the Cow Pose and exhale through the Cat Pose.

How to Do

Begin with your hands and knees in a tabletop position. You should make sure you align your shoulders above your wrists and your hips are aligned above your knees. Come to a horizontal back by lengthening the spine. Place your head and neck in a non-aligned position, staring down in the direction of the floor.

Breathe in and curve your back. Elevate through your glutes and the crown of your head and allow your belly to drop toward the floor. Rotate the shoulders up and down the back, feeling the back bend in your thoracic spine. Widen up your chest.

Hold the Cow Pose for one breath. Exhale and come back to a nonaligned, tabletop position again. You can also practice this in combination with the Cat Pose, alternating inhales with the Cow Pose and exhales with the Cat Pose.

Benefits

This is a gentle backbend that works with the Cat Pose to awaken the spine. Opens the chest, shoulders and upper back. Teaches the connection between inhaling and expanding and exhaling and contracting.

Tip

Care for your neck by widening your shoulder blades and pulling your shoulders down, away from your ears.

Butterfly Pose (Baddha Konasana)

The Butterfly Pose is a seated pose that strengthens and opens your hips and groin while decreasing abdominal pain.

How to Do

Sit with your knees near to your chest. Relax your knees out to each side and slightly press the bottoms of your feet together. Hold on to your ankles or feet.

Benefits

The Butterfly Pose is a good stretch for your inner thighs, groins, and knees. It helps improve the flexibility in your groin and hip area. When standing and walking for long hours, it removes fatigue.

Can give assistance from menstrual discomfort and menopause symptoms and smooth delivery if it's practiced on a regular basis until late pregnancy. Also helps in intestine and bowel movement.

Tips

You may find it difficult to lower your knees toward the floor. If your knees are incredibly high and your back is rounded, be sure to sit on a high support, even as high as a foot off the floor.

One Legged King Pigeon Pose (Eka Pada Rajakapotasana)

The One-Legged King Pigeon Pose typically known as the Pigeon Pose is a strong hip-opener that can help increase your flexibility and the scope of motion in your hip joints.

How to Do

Start off in Downward-Facing Dog pose, or on your hands and knees in the Table Pose. Bringing your left knee in the middle of your hands, place your left ankle close your right wrist. Lengthen your right leg behind you so that your kneecap and the top of your foot and toes lie on the floor.

Pushing with your fingertips, raise your upper body away from your thigh. Elongate the front of your body, while releasing your tailbone back toward your heels. Work on aligning your hips and the front side of your torso to the front of your mat.

Drawing down through your front-leg shin, balance out your weight equally in the middle of your right and left hips.

Flexing the front of your foot, press down through the tops of all five of your toes and the back of your foot, as you set your focus towards the floor.

Hold this pose for up to one minute. To release the pose, gather your back toes, raise your back knee off the mat, and then push yourself back into the Downward-Facing Dog. Repeat this pose for the equal amount of time on the other side.

Benefits

The One-Legged King Pigeon Pose stretches the thighs, groins, and abdomen. It can regularly be felt intensely in particular upper-leg and hip muscles. It eases tension in your chest and shoulders, as it additionally promotes the abdominal organs, which benefits your digestion management.

Tips

For added support, you may place a thickly folded towel or blanket beneath your hip.

Eagle Pose (Garudasana)

The Eagle Pose might seem like a crazy yoga pose; however, it's not so difficult if you break it down. Because you pull your limbs into the body with the knees bent, your center of gravity is low. It is a stability challenge since it's less unstable than many poses where you're standing on one leg.

How to Do

Stand up straight. Bend your knees, lift your left foot and cross your left thigh over the right. Hook the top of the left foot behind the right calf. Stretch your arms to the sides parallel to the floor. Bend your elbows and raise your forearms perpendicular to the floor. Put your right elbow over your left elbow and press your palms together. Look straight.

Benefits

The Eagle Pose strengthens and stretches your ankles and calves while stretching the shoulders, upper back, thighs, and hips. It can improve concentration and your sense of balance.

Tip

If you have trouble balancing on one leg, this pose can be done in a chair to help you stay upright or rest your backside on a wall. Also, put a block under the foot if you can't hook the lifted foot around the calf.

Bridge Pose (Setu Bandha Sarvangasana)

The Bridge Pose is a beginning backbend that helps to open your chest and stretch your thighs.

How to Do

To begin, lie supine (on your back). Fold your knees and keep your feet hip distance apart on the floor, ten to twelve inches from your pelvis, with your knees and ankles in a straight line. With your arms beside your body, place your palms faced down.

Breathe in, while slowly lifting your lower back, middle back and upper back off the floor. Gently roll in your shoulders. Touch your chest to your chin without bringing the chin down. Support your weight with your shoulders, arms, and feet. Feel your buttocks firm up in this pose. Both your thighs should be parallel to each other and to the floor.

You could interlock your fingers and push your hands on the floor to lift your torso a bit more up if you want or you could support your back with your palms. Keep breathing easily.

Hold this pose for a minute or two and then exhale as you gently release the pose.

Benefits

The Bridge Pose strengthens your back, opens the chest, and improves your spinal mobility.

Tips

After you roll your shoulders under, be sure not to pull them away from your ears. This often overstrains your neck. Raise the tops of your shoulders toward your ears and push your inner shoulder blades away from your spine.

Downward Facing Dog Pose (Adho Mukha Svanasana)

Downward Facing Dog Pose is one of the traditional Sun Salutation sequences poses. It's also an excellent yoga asana all on its own.

How to Do

Begin with your hands and knees in a tabletop position. Make sure your shoulders are aligned above your wrists and your hips are aligned above your knees. Come to a flat back by lengthening the spine. Place your head and neck in a non-aligned position, staring down in the direction of the floor.

Breathe out and raise your knees away from the floor. At the start, keep your knees slightly bent and your heels lifted away from the floor. Lengthen your tailbone positioned from the back of your pelvis and press it slightly toward the pubis. Alongside this tension, raise the resting bones in the direction of the ceiling, and from your inner ankles pull the inner legs up into the groin.

Followed by letting your breath out, push your top thighs back and extend your heels against or down toward the floor. Making sure that you do not lock them, straighten your knees and steady your outer thighs, rolling the upper thighs inward slightly, narrowing the front of the pelvis.

Firming the outer arms, press the bottoms of your index fingers assertively into the floor. From these two points, lift alongside the inside of your arms from the wrists to the tops of the shoulders. Firm your shoulder blades against your back then widen them and draw them toward the tailbone. Keep your head between your upper arms; not allowing it to simply hang.

Continue in this pose somewhere between one to three minutes. Afterward, bend your knees to the floor with a breath and repose in the Child's Pose.

Benefits

Downward Facing Dog pose can help decrease back pain through strengthening the whole back and shoulder girdle. It aids in stronger hands, wrists, the Achilles tendon, low-back, hamstrings, and calves, as well as increasing the full-body circulation. Elongates your shoulders and shoulder blade area. Decrease in tension and headaches by elongating the cervical spine and neck and relaxing the head. It can also lessen anxiety and expand your respiration

Tips

You can alleviate the burden on your wrists by employing a block beneath your palms or you can be capable of completing the pose upon your elbows. By lifting your hands on blocks or the seat of a chair, you can help to release and open your shoulders.

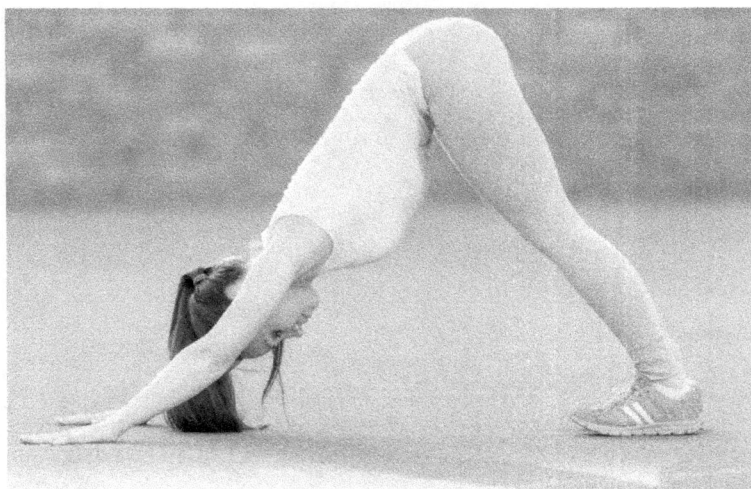

Seated Wide Angle Forward Fold Pose (Upavistha Konasana)

The Seated Wide Angle Forward Fold Pose is a seated yoga pose that deeply elongates your legs and spine, at the same time as calming your mind and releasing stress. It is commonly practiced just before the close of a yoga class, while your body is warm, to get ready your body for even deeper forward bends.

How to Do

Beginning from the Staff Pose, open your legs out as wide as it is comfortable for you. Keep your thighs engaged and your feet arched.

Make sure that your toes are pointing perpendicular to the ceiling as that is the best position for your hips and knees. Don't allow your feet to droop inward or open outward. Press your legs down into the floor.

Breathe in and position down by way of your bottom. Breathe out and forward bend by moving your pelvis forward. Maintain this repetition on each inhale and exhale to deepen the pose.

Let your arms come straight out in front of you and keep your stare softy at the floor to prevent turning your neck.

Benefits

Stimulates your abdominal organs, strengthens the back, stretches your inner thighs and hamstrings and soothes your nervous system.

Tips

Seated Wide Angle Forward Fold Pose is a challenging forward bend for many beginners. If you have trouble bending even a fraction forward, it's okay to bend your knees to some extent. You may possibly even support your knees on rolled blankets or supports; just remember, as you start into the forward bend, it's still essential to keep your kneecaps pointing upwards.

Lizard Pose (Utthan Pristhasana)

The Lizard Pose is a powerful hip opener and can produce some intense sensation.

How to Do

Start in Downward Facing Dog Pose. Step with your left foot forward in the middle of your palms, keeping your hands on the floor. Lowering your right knee to the floor, release your elbows to the floor as well. You can either bring your hands together in prayer position or rest your hands, palms facing down on the mat.

Keep on squeezing your left knee to your body and keep your focus in front of you to urge your hips to lower toward the floor. Remain here for at least five breaths. At that point, come back onto your hands. Fold your back toes and step your left leg back. Take a moment and move your right foot forward to do this pose on the other side.

Benefits

The Lizard Pose opens the chest, hips, and hamstrings.

Tip

Not recommended for those suffering from bad knee, or back conditions.

Plow Pose (Halasana)

The Plow Pose prepares the sphere of your body and mind for a deep transformation.

How to Do

Lie on your backside and bend your legs. While keeping your legs together, set your feet on the floor. Raise your feet and pelvis from the floor. You can assist with your hands, and lower your knees onto your forehead. You can then press your palms against your back or clasp your hands and lower them on the floor behind your back. Go back, rolling your spine back on the floor to release.

Benefits

The Plow Pose opens your neck, shoulders, and back. By compressing your abdomen, it massages and tones your digestive organs, which increases your body's cleansing. This pose promotes and regulates your thyroid gland, helps get rid of excess mucus and phlegm, and regulates your breath.

Tip

With this pose, you may have an inclination to overtax your neck by straining your shoulders too far away from your ears. As the tops of your shoulders should push down into the support, they should be raised toward the ears to keep the back of your neck and throat soft. Open your sternum by compressing the shoulder blades against your back.

Corpse Pose (Shavasana)

The Corpse Pose is typically performed at the end of a yoga sequence. It can on the other hand be utilized at the start to calm your body before performing or in the midpoint of a sequence to rest. When applied at the conclusion of a yoga practice it is usually followed by a seated meditation phase to re-incorporate the body mind spirit back into the world.

How to Do

Lying on your back let your arms and legs drop open. With your arms at about forty five degrees from the side of your body, make sure you are comfortable and warm. With your eyes closed begin with slow deep breaths through the nose.

Allowing your entire body to become soft and heavy, let it relax onto the floor. As your body relaxes, feel your full body expanding and decreasing with each breath. Glance over your body from your toes to the top of your head, inspecting for any tension, stiffness or tightened muscles. Intentionally let go and relax any spots that you may find. Sway or shake those parts of your body from side to side to boost further release.

Let go of all control of your breath, your mind, and your body. Allow your body to move deeper and further into a state of complete relaxation. Remain in the Corpse Pose for five to fifteen minutes.

To release the Corpse Pose gradually deepen your breath, wriggle your fingers and toes, bring your arms over your head and stretch your entire body, breathing out, bend your knees into your chest, then roll over to one side going into the fetal position. Once you are ready, slowly inhaling, rising up into a seated position.

Benefits

The Corpse Pose allows your body and mind the time to sort out what has occurred during a yoga session. To most individuals, no yoga session is finished without this final pose. Your body needs this time to comprehend the new information it has received during the practice of yoga. Even though the Corpse Pose is a resting pose, you are not going to sleep.

Tips

Simply, relax. Follow your breathing without striving to control it. Observe what's taking place in your body. Gather your thoughts as they come along and let them go.

Chair Pose (Utkatasana)

The Chair Pose is a standing yoga posture that tones your entire body. The Chair Pose is an important component of Sun Salutations and is also often used as a transitional pose. It can also be practiced on its own to help build strength and stamina through your entire body.

How to Do

Begin with the Mountain Pose. Your big toes should be in contact of each other and your heels should be fixed a little apart. Your lower belly has to be drawn in a little to help support your spine. Move your shoulder blades downward keep your chest open and pushed out across your shoulders.

Take a deep breath and raise your arms over your head. You can keep your arms parallel to each other or just keep them up with the palms joined, facing inward. Your arms should be held at the same height or in front of your ears.

Bring your lower ribs toward your pelvis. At that point, breathe out and bend your knees. Try to make your thighs as parallel to the floor as you can. Your knees should come out in front of your feet. The torso should lean a little forward over the thighs till the torso makes a right angle with the upper part of the thighs. Your inner thighs should be parallel to each other and they should push the tops of your thigh bones to the heels.

Keep the edges of your shoulders firm. Bring your tailbone downward to the ground and towards your pubic bone to extend your lower back.

Remain in this pose for thirty seconds to one minute. To release, straighten your knees while you breathe in. Afterward, breathe out and bring your arms to the sides of your body, back into the Mountain Pose.

Benefits

The Chair pose exercises the spine, hips and chest muscles. It also helps to strengthen the lower back, torso and toning the thigh, ankle, leg and knee muscles.

Tips

Practice this near a wall to help you remain in the pose. You can stand with your back near the wall just a few inches away from it. Keep a proper distance to when you come into position, your tailbone comes into contact it then supported by the wall.

Warrior Three Pose (Virabhadrasana III)

The Warrior Three Pose is an intermediate balancing pose in yoga. This energetic standing posture builds stability throughout your whole body by incorporating all of the muscles through your core, arms, and legs.

How to Do

Begin in the Mountain Pose. With an exhale, move your right foot back about two feet, as you maintain your body weight forward on your left foot. Keep your left toes looking forward. Feel your left toes spread and find an even basis through the sole of your left foot. Put your hands on your hips to bring into line your hips and shoulders perpendicular to the front of your mat. Tighten your inner core muscles by pulling in the navel and waist.

Maintain a feeling you are holding the lower organs with a round band of muscle, then breathe in and raise your right foot as your incline your torso forward experiencing a hinging movement at your hips. Direct your stare straight down as you bend forward from your hips attaining a new focus.

As your torso and right leg go into a corresponding position with the floor, lengthen both legs without bracing into the bottom knee. The right hip may rise higher than the left. Keeping your right hip level with the left hip, experience a shift in a correct postural alignment. Imagine more length advancing into the right leg and spine. Maintain the digging into the left foot and tightening into the core muscles.

To intensify the influence of the balance, free your hands from your hips and elongate your arms straight out to the sides expanding your chest or forward in line with your head and neck. If you extend your arms forward, then turn your palms to face each other so your shoulder blades can draw down away from your ears. Breathe and stay here for five to ten breaths.

To release this pose, inhale as you lift your chest and place your right foot back into Mountain Pose. Exhale as you lower your arms, and draw a few breaths as you pause and then repeat on the right side for the same time.

Benefits

The Warrior III pose strengthens your legs, improves balance and your core strength.

Tips

You can either stand in front of the wall, bringing your arms outstretched in front of you with your hands on the wall or rotate and bring the raised back foot onto the wall. Both will give you the stability you require to level your hips. You can also hold on a chair as a substitute for using the wall.

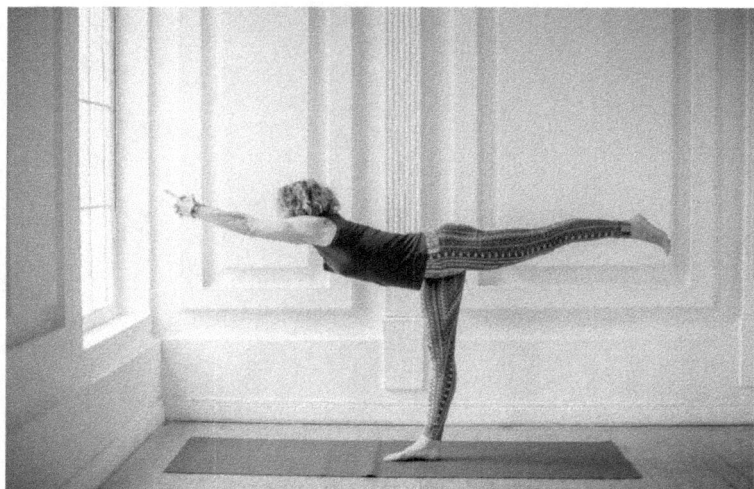

Constructing a Yoga Sequence

Here are a few points to keep in mind how to construct a yoga sequence. You are not at a studio, paying to be there. You do not have to exercise for over an hour. Begin with 5-10 minutes. Notice how you feel by the end of this time. If you feel as if you can do more, go ahead. If no, end your routine there.

Start with 5-10 minutes. By the conclusion of that time, notice how you feel. Do you desire to resume? If yes, continue for an extra five minutes and then check in with yourself once more. If not, close your workout.

The same as any physical journey, a yoga sequence has three clear parts.

Your opening or warm-up sequence

You don't want to jump into the main event tight and cold. This is where you move through and loosening up your major muscle groups as well as body parts

Your main sequence

Once you've warmed up, it's time for your main sequence. This component of your sequence is influenced by the goal of your routine. If it's an asymmetrical pose, keep in mind to do both sides and devote about the same time on each side.

The closing or cool down sequence

Now you've completed the principal portion of your yoga practice, it's time to cool down.

About The Author

Monique Joiner Siedlak is a writer, witch, and warrior on a mission to awaken people to their greatest potential through the power of storytelling infused with mysticism, modern paganism, and new age spirituality. At the young age of 12, she began rigorously studying the fascinating philosophy of Wicca. By the time she was 20, she was self-initiated into the craft, and hasn't looked back ever since. To this day, she has authored over 35 books pertaining to the magick and mysteries of life. Her most recent publication is book one of an Urban Paranormal series entitled "Jaeger Chronicles."

Originally from Long Island, New York, Monique is now a proud inhabitant of Northeast Florida; however, she considers herself to be a citizen of Mother Earth. When she doesn't have a book or pen in hand, she loves exploring new places and learning new things. And being the nature lover that she is, she considers herself to be an avid animal advocate.

To find out more about Monique Joiner Siedlak artistically, spiritually, and personally, feel free to visit her **official website**.

Other Books by Monique Joiner Siedlak

Mojo's Wiccan Series

Wiccan Basics

Candle Magick

Wiccan Spells

Love Spells

Abundance Spells

Hoodoo

Herb Magick

Seven African Powers: The Orishas

Moon Magick

Cooking for the Orishas

Creating Your Own Spells

Body Mind and Soul Series

Creative Visualization

Astral Projection for Beginners

Meditation for Beginners

Reiki for Beginners

Thorne Witch Series

The Phoenix

Beautiful You Series

Creating Your Own Body Butter

Creating Your Own Body Scrub

Creating Your Own Body Spray

Mojo's Self-Improvement Series

Manifesting With the Law of Attraction

Stress Management

Jaeger Chronicles

Glen Cove

Connect With Me!

I really appreciate you reading my book! Please leave a review and let me know your thoughts. Here are the social media locations you can find me at:

Like my Facebook Page: www.facebook.com/mojosiedlak

Follow me on Twitter: www.twitter.com/mojosiedlak

Follow me on Instagram: www.instagram.com/mojosiedlak

Follow me on Bookbub: http://bit.ly/2KEMkqt

Sign up to my Email List at www.mojosiedlak.com and receive a free book!

If you enjoyed this book or found it useful I'd be very grateful if you'd post a short review at your retailer. Your support really does make a difference and I read all the reviews personally so I can get your feedback and make this as well as the next book even better.

www.ingramcontent.com/pod-product-compliance
Lightning Source LLC
Chambersburg PA
CBHW071636040426
42452CB00009B/1645